31 PRAYERS FOR PROSPERITY

31 Prayers for Prosperity

EVIE LAWSON

EV Publishing LLC

Copyright © 2021 by Evie Lawson

All rights reserved. No part of this book may be reproduced in any manner whatsoever without written permission except in the case of brief quotations embodied in critical articles and reviews.

First Printing, 2021

This book is dedicated to my beautiful
grandmother,
Georgia Lawson.

INTRODUCTION

There is a reason why you are reading these words right now. The reason may be that you are interested in the interior material of the book. The reason may be because you want to pass the time. The reason may even be the fact that someone gave you this book as a gift. Whatever the reason is, all that matters is that you have now started the spiritual journey that will undoubtedly change your life.

Praying, by definition, is the act of speaking to a spiritual entity privately or amongst others to express love, appreciation, recognition, or to ask for something in particular. The act of prayer can provide the individual the hope and confidence needed to overcome the relevant circumstances they may be encountering. Even though praying is a conversation with an entity that may not be tangible, it is a beneficial activity that can lead to happiness, courage, and peace of mind.

This book provides thirty-one prosperity prayers that ignite the spiritual journey needed for anyone attempting to receive the happiness, courage, and peace of mind mentioned earlier. Because of the comprehension of different religions, the author refers to the spiritual being as the Universal Energy. To get the most out of this book, the reader has to believe that prayer changes things and recite at least one prayer per day. This particular act of faith will provide the reader with a new sense of confidence. The type of confidence that will allow the individual to go through life with a sense of control and purpose. The reader must also be informed that the author did not compose this text on his own but with the assistance of the almighty universal energy referred to throughout this book. Without further a due, the author presents to you 31 Prayers for Prosperity.

THE FIRST PRAYER

Dear Almighty Universal Energy, I come to you at this moment to tell you that I love you. I come to you knowing whatever I ask of you; your holy spirit will provide not because you have to but because you have unlimited grace. I humbly require your supernatural guidance in granting me financial freedom. I pray that you raise me from the grips of inability and that you grant me money, happiness, and peace of mind so I can share your blessings with not only myself but my family and fellow people. I thank you for being with me no matter what. Thank you for bringing me this far in life; you have shown me mercy even though I have committed sinful actions. I pray your blessings are so abundant that I will never have to want anything but your everlasting relationship. I pray in your name, Amen.

THE SECOND PRAYER

I come to you the almighty Universal Energy, my protector, my guide, my savior. I am praying for forgiveness and favor. Present to me your faithful ways for me to prosper in all I do, no matter how big or small. I want to thank you in advance for blessing me with the opportunity of attaining prosperity. Your love is everlasting, and your grace is amazing. Warm my heart and produce happiness in my life now and forever. I pray in your name, Amen.

THE THIRD PRAYER

Almighty and Everlasting Energy, I come to you as humbly as I know how with my eyes closed and my heart open. Thank you for everything you have done for me and everything you will do for me in the future. I am in a situation where I need your help with my finances. It has been written that If I ask you for what I need and thank you for what you have done, you will demonstrate your abundant grace and mercy. I ask for wealth to not only ensure my financial freedom but to be able to bless others. Thank you for receiving my prayer and giving me hope when all hope was lost. I love you so much, and I know you will grant my humble prayer. I pray in your name, Amen.

THE FOURTH PRAYER

Dear almighty one, I pray to you at this moment to express gratitude for everything you have done for me. I realize that I am now worthy and deserving of your wealth and accomplishment. Thank you for helping me understand that you provide more than enough funds for everyone. Your grace enables numerous channels of wealth to be allowable. I plead for your unlimited charity to inevitably provide the continuation of appreciation, achievement, pleasure, peace, and prosperity to flow effortlessly into my life consistently. Once again, thank you for everything, and I pray this prayer in your name, Amen.

THE FIFTH PRAYER

Dear divine one, I pray to you for help with my financial situation at this moment because I understand prosperity and wealth only come from you. I genuinely believe you regulate everything desirable; it does not matter if it is finances, employment opportunities, academic possibilities, or peace of mind; you can provide it all. I know there is nothing I cannot request from you, almighty one. Thank you for providing wealth and prosperity in my life and allowing me the opportunity to bless others. It is written that if we believe and have complete trust in you, your blessings will be abundant and everlasting. Thank you for possessing the listening ear that I desperately need right now. I love you so much, and I pray in your name, Amen.

THE SIXTH PRAYER

I come to you, at this specific moment, to ask for assistance in regards to my financial situation. I genuinely believe you can immediately assist me in my time of trouble because you are almighty, all-powerful, and graceful. It is written that you shall provide all my needs as long as I have faith in your name.

Forgive me for all of my inadequacies, and forgive those who have hurt me in the past. I ask you not to let my past transgressions hinder me from enjoying a life of abundance, happiness, and peace of mind.

Thank you, almighty one, for bringing me this far, and thank you for hearing these words and acting on them. You have never let me down, and I know you will not let me down now.

I also want to thank you for the opportunity to fix my financial situation, my relationships with other people, and my business endeavors. I shall never forget the many times you have extended your favor on not only my life but the many people in this world. Thank you for being a shoulder to cry on and a listening ear that is always available. I love you so much, and I invoke this prayer in your name, Amen.

THE SEVENTH PRAYER

Dear superior energy, I want to thank you for the opportunity to obtain prosperity and financial blessings. I can genuinely say you have blessed me tremendously by providing all I could ever ask for by being a loyal friend, guide, and supplier.

Thank you for granting me complete knowledge and wisdom. Thank you for transforming my past failures into today's success. I also want to thank you for changing my unfavorable circumstances into positive ones. You promised that you would never leave or forsake me, and you have undoubtedly kept your word. I love you so much, and I recite this prayer in your name, Amen.

THE EIGHTH PRAYER

Dear all-knowing universal energy, I recite this prayer because I need your strength and unconditional devotion. Your detailed attention to my life has been the only thing keeping me alive and well. I want to thank you for your favor in regards to my finances, health, and relationships. Almighty one, continue to provide hope, wealth, and opportunities for not only me but for my fellow man. Allow your spirit to overtake my mind, so the only thing I will desire is your love and blessings. Be with me, and hear my prayer from not my mouth but my heart. I recite this prayer in your name, Amen.

THE NINTH PRAYER

Boundless spiritual energy, I am praying to you at this moment to give you thanks for all of the harmony, pleasure, peace, wellness, independence, and blessings you have bestowed upon me throughout life. I am thankful for the opportunity to be a vital part of your unlimited life force, and I am incredibly blessed to be a product of your overwhelming grace.

By reciting this prayer to you, I want to thank you for listening to me when I asked you for absolute peace, complete love, and blessed prosperity. I genuinely believe my past prayers to you regarding my financial freedom have now become tangible health, wealth, and time that I can now enjoy in this lifetime. You have provided me with everything anyone could ever need to enjoy life thoroughly. I declare accomplishment and wealth in my life, and I thank you for the opportunity to help others.

I'm so grateful for everything you have done for my loved ones and me, and I pray you will never leave nor forsake me. I recite this prayer in your name, Amen.

THE TENTH PRAYER

Dear almighty, all-knowing, all righteous one, I am coming to you at this moment to ask you for help with my finances, debt relief, and all other financial responsibilities.

Throughout the years, I have made countless financial mistakes. In the past, I have mismanaged my funds, acquired debt, and now my monetary problems have become out of control. I ask for your forgiveness and grace regarding my poor financial judgments. I pray you bring me out of this predicament and bless me with abundance and happiness.

I know I can always come to you, no matter the issue, and I know you will help me overcome each trial, every tribulation. I know you can make a way out of no way. That is why I am giving you thanks in advance for the upcoming financial breakthrough in my life.

Thank you for bestowing upon me the opportunity to overcome my past bad judgments, and thank you for allowing me to learn from those previous failures. Thank you for all the financial opportunities and profitable business ventures that you will present to me in the upcoming future. Thank you for humbling me, so I may not depend on monetary things but on your unlimited grace. I love you, and I pray this prayer in your name, Amen.

THE ELEVENTH PRAYER

My superior energy, I love you, and I need you during this time in my life. I know I am not supposed to worry about anything but pray about everything, and that is what I am doing now. I am coming to you because I need your grace and blessings regarding income improvement, financial success, health, and genuine peace in my life.

Furthermore, I want to thank you for everything you have done so far in my life, and I want to thank you for everything you are going to do for me in the future. I want to thank you for keeping me safe from injury and harm. I also want to thank you for being a loyal friend, I love you, and I pray this prayer in your name, Amen.

THE TWELFTH PRAYER

O Superior Unlimited Energy, I pray that you encourage and renew my soul. Refine my spirit and mind so that I may be in total harmony with you and your unconditional grace. Even in past situations where I may have been going through various difficulties and hopelessness, you have consistently had my back and helped me overcome those circumstances every time.

Because of your blessings and favor, I no longer experience sorrow or grief but hope and peace. Your love and compassion have allowed me to enjoy financial freedom and harmony in relationships with others genuinely. I beg you almighty energy to never leave my side, and I pray you forgive me for all of the sins I have committed in the past. I love you, and I pray this prayer in your name, Amen.

THE THIRTEENTH PRAYER

Universal Energy, I know you are all-powerful, forgiving, and graceful. I ask at this moment for your understanding and blessing. Allow your glory to oversee my finances, time on this earth, gifts, and all of my fellow people. I genuinely believe everything comes from you, and it is written that you will never leave nor forsake me.

Thank you for everything you have done for me and everything you will do for me in the future. Forgive me for everything I have done wrong and acknowledge all my good deeds. I love you, and I recite this prayer in your name, Amen.

THE FOURTEENTH PRAYER

I understand that everything within the universe exists because of your boundless energy. Evidence of your unlimited power exists in your conceptions of the sun, nature, and human life. Without your divine energy, no being can ever prevail in this world. I want to take this time to praise you for all the great things you created that make our lives significant and deserving of continuation.

Please continue to provide regular meals, adequate shelter, and financial resources so that my loved ones and I may live a life of fulfillment and abundance. I do not want to live a life of mediocrity but one of ample financial rewards. I believe I am worthy of your blessings, and I pray you believe the same thing.

Thank you for the past peace, prosperity, and happiness you have bestowed upon me throughout my life. I know nothing happens without your transcendent blessings, and I thank you for listening to this prayer. I recite this prayer in your name, Amen.

THE FIFTEENTH PRAYER

Dear divine energy, I address you at this time with a pure heart and an open mind. I need your divine grace now more than ever. I specifically ask you to provide me with an excess of funds from your eternal source.

Your direction and guidance are all I need during this period of life. I comprehend that I will never understand your techniques, but I realize that your blessings are always on time. Your financial guidance is needed, and I trust you will come thru for your loyal servant.

I have ultimate faith in your name and your power. I pray you realize how much you mean to me and the unconditional love I have for you. Your name means everything to me as I recite this prayer in your name, AMEN!

THE SIXTEENTH PRAYER

Universal Energy, I recite this prayer to you because I genuinely believe you will eliminate financial trouble from my life. I come to you now to pray for your monetary blessing and your drastic advances in all aspects of my life.

My confidence in you is excellent, and I know you will render my people and me all of your abundant blessings. Money is nothing compared to your grace, and I understand that faith in your works will provide all of the financial resources I need.

Furthermore, I want to thank you for relieving my financial distress, debt responsibilities and alleviating the stressful situations in life I had to endure. I also want to thank you for assisting me in all of my decision-making. Thank you for all of the past, present, and future opportunities you have and will bless me with in the future. Thank you for everything; I recite this prayer in your name, Amen.

THE SEVENTEENTH PRAYER

I proceed to chant this invocation to claim many financial blessings for not only myself but for everyone who believes in your grace. My confidence in your overwhelming blessings keeps me content because I know that no matter what may happen to me in life, you will undoubtedly provide for not only me but anyone who believes in your power.

I ask you to provide me the discernment not to seek unnecessary luxuries but the comprehension to acquire monetary materials that will prove beneficial to my financial situation. I want to thank you in advance for the opportunity to relieve my financial woes and overcome any stressful situation.

I thank you for providing the courage to praise your name and broadcast your love. Your listening ear is always available; therefore, this prayer is in your name, Amen.

THE EIGHTEENTH PRAYER

Dear Superior Energy, I need your assistance in obtaining peace and happiness, especially at this moment in life. I will do everything in my power to trust you because I know you are capable of all things. I know you can change any unfavorable situation into a favorable one.

Allow me to wake up every morning appreciative of the fact that I am on this earth another day. Give me hope that your plan for me will deliver abundance and peace of mind. Please guide me physically, mentally, and emotionally so that I can realize harmony, accomplishment, and pleasure in life.

I have faith in the idea that your blessings will satisfy all of my desires. I love you, and I thank you for everything. I pray this prayer in your name Amen.

THE NINETEENTH PRAYER

The almighty, all-knowing, and all-graceful one, I put all my concerns in your care, and I pray to you at this moment for your overflowing prosperity. I pray for the knowledge and wisdom needed to live a financially free lifestyle.

I acknowledge that you are the source of everything good, plentiful, and beneficial. I want to thank you in advance for providing my spirit with determination, concentration, and discernment. I also want to thank you in advance for all of the opportunities you will provide for me. These opportunities will give me the platform to express to others your grace and mercy.

I love you so much, and I thank you for everything you have done for me and everything you will do for me. Bless us all, and continue to bestow your favor on not only me but also my fellow people. I pray in your name, Amen.

THE TWENTIETH PRAYER

Dear Unlimited Energy, I want to start this prayer off by thanking you for all of the previous blessings you have bestowed on me. Even though I have had my moments of scarcity in the past, you have always made a way out of no way, and I want to thank you for your grace. If I had unlimited tongues, I could not thank you enough for being there for me in my time of need. I am now in need of your financial grace once more.

I pray that once you bestow my bank account with monetary gains, I will have the knowledge and wisdom to not be selfish or irresponsible in utilizing the provided funds. I also pray that you help me use these funds to take care of my immediate needs, eliminate debt, and give glory to your name.

Thank you for taking the time to listen to my request. You said you would never neglect nor abandon me, and I believe in that with all of my mind, body, and soul. I love you immensely, and I recite this prayer in your name, Amen.

THE TWENTYFIRST PRAYER

I recite this prayer to you at this particular moment to attain prosperity and stability from your overwhelming well of blessings. It is written that you are my protector, my guide, and my leader, and I believe every word of that statement. I ask you to provide me with the courage, knowledge, and faith needed to succeed in everything I do while living on this earthly plane.

I pray for your help to thrive financially, mentally, and emotionally. Once I ask you for these things, I know you will provide for me, and I want to thank you in advance for being the loyal friend you are. Thank you for all the blessings you have bestowed upon me in the past and for all the blessings you will provide for me in the future. I love you very much, and I pray this prayer in your name, Amen.

THE TWENTY-SECOND PRAYER

Dear Supreme Energy, I ask from you at this moment your favor. Your favor in granting me the experience of living a happy and prosperous life.

I ask you to renew my understanding of satisfaction and allow your divine energy to live in my mind. Without your assistance, I am bound to fail, but I can live the life I was meant to live with your guidance.

My love for you is unconditional, and my faith in your timing is unlimited. Eliminate all thoughts of stress and fill my mind with thoughts of positivity. I praise you for being there for me in the past, being a present ear, and being the reason I have hope in the future. Once again, I want to express my love for you, and I recite this prayer in your name, Amen.

The Twenty-Third Prayer

Superior Energy, I require your kindness & empathy. Please excuse all of my shortcomings and forgive the individuals who have transgressed against me. I ask of you to remove any form of debt from my life and bestow upon abundance.

Grant my loved ones and me adequate finances so that we will be able to meet our everyday needs. Allmighty one, I also pray for a life full of excellent health and peace of mind.

Thank you for listening to this prayer. I know I can call upon you at any time, and I am incredibly thankful for that opportunity. Thank you for everything you have done for me in the past and everything you will do for me in the future. I love you, and I pray this prayer in your name, Amen.

THE TWENTY-FOURTH PRAYER

Universal Energy, I pray to you at this time because I know your grace and glory are unquestionable. I ask for you to take complete control of my thoughts, body, and spirit so I may live a life of truth and abundance. I need Your divine help. I need your assistance in living the life I was meant to live.

Forgive me for my sins so I may live a life of peace and not conflict. Thank you for allowing me to conversate with you another day. I know nothing is more remarkable than you and your faithful blessings. Thank you for giving me hope when all hope was lost. I love you, and I pray you will never forget your loyal servant. I announce this prayer in your name, Amen.

THE TWENTY-FIFTH PRAYER

Beloved energy, I seek your guidance and wisdom in this time of need. I understand that if I pray to you with complete faith, your blessings will shower over my life. I comprehend your power and your unlimited grace; that is why I am asking your energy to transform my life.

I ask for financial relief and consistent peace of mind. Thank you for being there for me in the past, and I know you will allow me to enjoy my future. Without you in could do nothing, but with your favor, I can do all things. I love you, and I recite this prayer in your name, Amen.

THE TWENTY-SIXTH PRAYER

I read these words with the confidence to know you will answer this prayer. This is my humble prayer to you, the almighty energy, in hopes of living a better life. I need you more than ever, and I know your grace is everlasting. Take over my finances so I may be able to fulfill my everyday obligations.

Take my transgressions and make them my testimony. Take my negatives and make them my positives. I know every prayer communicated to you will be answered, and I am incredibly grateful. Please guide me on my walk of life; let me not stumble but run through the obstacles. I love you, and I pray this prayer in your name, Amen.

THE TWENTY-SEVENTH PRAYER

Dear Universal Energy, I come to you at this time with the expectation of your glory bestowing upon my communicated words. I understand my prayer will be fulfilled because you are the creator of miracles and always a consistent shoulder to lean on. My prayers usually consist of me asking you for something but this particular prayer is to give you praises and thanks.

Thank you for being something I can believe in, especially in a world where it seems like everyone lets me down time and time again. Thank you for providing me your word in which I can refer to in times of confusion and hopelessness. I have a tremendous amount of gratitude for your blessings, even though I have sinned in the past. Your grace is not judgemental, nor is it unlimited.

I believe in your tremendous power and your overwhelming love. I love you so much, and I recite this prayer in your name, Amen.

THE TWENTY-EIGHTH PRAYER

Allmighty Energy, I ask you for the opportunity to grow closer to you. I ask for you to be the loyal friend I never had. I pray you will not judge me for my past acts but recognize me for my willingness to live better. I know I am not perfect, nor do I try to be, because I know you are the only perfect being. Please listen to this prayer and share your blessings upon my words.

Allow me to dismiss negative thoughts and fill my mind with your capabilities. Allow me not to worry about life circumstances but seek your guidance in every situation I may encounter.

Thank you for providing me with the resources needed to live a more prosperous, peaceful, and hopeful life. Thank you for allowing me to see the sunrise again and the darkness of the night. Thank you for everything you have done for me. If I had a million tounges, I could not thank you enough. I love you, and thank you for taking the time to hear my words. In your mighty name, I pray, Amen.

THE TWENTY-NINTH PRAYER

Universal energy, I understand that my communication with you is sacred and uncertain. I know I am praying to you to obtain a specific change, even though I can not physically see you. However, I know that every prayer I present to you will be answered, and you will hear every word I utter.

I ask you to satisfy my soul with positive energy so I may live a life of happiness and hope. I need your love, guidance, and forgiveness so I may overcome all obstacles presented to me. Your grace is powerful enough to transform not only my life but everyone who believes in your capabilities.

Thank you for allowing my prayer to be a powerful tool I can use to receive all the blessings you have available. Thank you for bestowing upon me the ability to demonstrate patience, courage, and action. Thank you for allowing my heart to accept your divine love, maturity, and abundance. I also want to thank you for every breath my lungs intake because I would not have any chance of life without it.

I love you more than anything. This prayer comes from my mind, my body, and my soul. I recite these words in your name, Amen.

THE THIRTIETH PRAYER

I come to you now because I have no doubt my prayer will be answered, and I am in desperate need of your unlimited favor. I am praying to you in hopes of you blessing me with wisdom, judgment, knowledge, comprehension, guidance, and control in all circumstances of life.

Thank you for allowing your blessings to rain down on me so I may achieve success in my relationships, goal achievement, financial transactions, and numerous life predicaments. Thank you for revealing the benefits of displaying honesty, virtue, faith, love, self-control, gratitude, compassion, confidence, dignity, and determination.

I can not make the words out to explain how much I love you and how appreciative I am for having you as a supporter. Thank you for everything, and I recite this prayer in your name, Amen.

THE THIRTYFIRST PRAYER

I come to you the almighty, the everlasting, the all-knowing being in the most humble way possible, with my heart open and my life dependent. It is written that you will answer my prayers as long as I believe, and I want you to know that I have absolute faith in your grace.

I am tired of going through poverty. I am tired of dealing with loneliness. I am done with looking at the mirror and not being satisfied with the reflection I see. I am sick of not having control of the undesirable life circumstances I deal with consistently.

I ask you to show me who you are. I am asking you to deliver me from this negativity. I am asking you to change my life in a way that I will have no other choice but to give you the praise you deserve.

Am I not important enough for your glory? Am I not a product of your image. Am I destined to live a life of sorrow, or am I a living testimony of your unbelievable potential? I demand an answer.

I am not trying to be disrespectful, but I want you to know I need you. I need you to shine a light on the darkness of my life. I need your blessings now more than ever.

Please hear my prayer and acknowledge my emotions. I love you more than anything else in the world. Please take all of my problems and transform them into answers. Take my hopelessness and transfer it to hope. Take my aspirations and transform them into tangible accomplishments. I pray this prayer in your name, Amen.

ABOUT THE AUTHOR

The author Evie Lawson is a United States Marine Corps veteran that was raised in Greensboro, Alabama. Mr. Lawson has obtained two bachleors degrees, one In Enterpreuship and another in Real Estate Studies. Mr. Lawson also has a masters degree in Business.

www.ingramcontent.com/pod-product-compliance
Lightning Source LLC
Chambersburg PA
CBHW071846290426
44109CB00017B/1947